EMOTIONAL LITERACY
Pocketbook

By James Park &
Marilyn Tew

Published by:

Teachers' Pocketbooks
Laurel House, Station Approach,
Alresford, Hampshire SO24 9JH, UK
Tel: +44 (0)1962 735573
Fax: +44 (0)1962 733637
E-mail: sales@teacherspocketbooks.co.uk
Website: www.teacherspocketbooks.co.uk

Teachers' Pocketbooks is an imprint of
Management Pocketbooks Ltd.

With thanks to Brin Best for his help in
launching the series.

This edition published 2007. Reprinted 2009.

ISBN 978 1903776 803

British Library Cataloguing-in-Publication
Data – A catalogue record for this book is
available from the British Library.

Design, typesetting and graphics by **Efex Ltd**.
Printed in UK.

Contents

Foreword

This is a book about how you can make your life as a teacher even more enjoyable and fulfilling, and how you can make learning even more fun for your students.

It shows how you can use emotional literacy to:

- Understand better what's really going on for young people in your class
- Become more effective at providing what they need if they are to learn
- Help them to grow, while at the same time looking after yourself

We hope it will convince you that emotional literacy is:

- Common sense rather than rocket science
- Not difficult to practise when you have other people on your side
- Something you definitely want to embrace in your teaching

Introduction

What is emotional literacy?

Emotional literacy is often defined as a **set of skills**. One commonly-used definition describes it as:

> The ability to recognise, understand, handle and appropriately express emotions.

Other people prefer to define it as a **set of practices**:

> The practice of thinking individually and collectively about how emotions shape our actions, and of using emotional understanding to enrich our thinking.

> The practice of interacting with people in ways that lead to a better understanding of our own and others' emotions, then using this understanding to inform our actions.

Both types of definition are useful in helping us to understand what happens in classrooms and for working out how to intervene to support learning.

What are emotional literacy skills?

If we think about emotional literacy as a set of skills, those skills can be divided into two groups: skills that relate to how we manage ourselves and skills that relate to how we manage our relationships with others.

Managing ourselves

- Can we cope with challenge, uncertainty and risk?

- Can we direct our actions in purposeful ways?

- Can we use our creativity?

- Can we make good decisions?

Managing our relationships

- Do we communicate what we want to the people in our lives?

- Do we get the most out of social interactions?

- Do we understand other people and what they are communicating to us?

- Do we create positive energy in our dealings with others?

An advantage of thinking about emotional literacy in this way is that individual skills and groups of skills can be taught. We can all become more proficient in managing ourselves and our relationships.

What are emotionally literate practices?

If we prefer to think of emotional literacy as a set of practices, these too can be divided, into practices that involve just us and those that involve us in relation to other people.

Individual practices

- Do we ask ourselves what we are feeling?

- Do we look for patterns in our emotional responses and think about how they affect the way we behave?

- Do we think about how we can respond most appropriately to different situations?

Relational practices

- Do we take an interest in what other people are feeling?

- Do we invite people to tell us why they respond as they do?

- Do we work at building relationships with other people?

Thinking about emotional literacy as a set of practices encourages us to think beyond the individual and to take in the whole situation. How things are organised and how we conduct ourselves impact upon our students' ability to manage their emotions.

How to use this book

Whether we think about it as a skill or a practice, emotional literacy enables us to get the best out of ourselves and other people. This book will help you to think about the principles of emotional literacy and use the information to:

- Appreciate how emotions affect learning (pp 12-28)
- Shape relationships that support learning (pp 29-38)
- Hold open conversations in your classrooms (pp 39-58)
- Organise things so as to make such conversations more likely (pp 59-70)
- Build cohesive and productive groups (pp 71-94)
- Enable students to tell better stories about themselves that allow them to change the way they learn (pp 95-106)
- Develop emotional literacy in the staffroom (pp 107-122)

On pages 123 and 124 you will find a set of overarching principles for emotional literacy, followed by some useful resources, further reading and websites.

Emotions and Learning

Feelings are important

In 1848, a building worker called Phineas Gage was involved in an accident that drove an iron bar through his brain. Despite this horrific injury, Gage survived. Not only that, he appeared, at first, to be largely unaffected. Greeted as a walking, talking miracle, he could recognise objects, remember his past life and do calculations much as he had always done.

He was, however, unable to have a relationship, consider options or make decisions. The damage he had sustained to an area at the front of his brain cut the links to the centres of emotional activity. This rendered him increasingly difficult, fitful and wilful.

The neuroscientist Antonio Damasio, who tells this story in his book *Descartes' Error*, concludes from it that you cannot think about anything important without having access to your emotions.

Why learners need feelings

The need to access feelings applies as much to the children and young people
who sit in our classrooms as it did to Phineas Gage. Learners use feelings to help them:

- Acquire, retain and recall information
- Build relationships that support and stimulate learning
- Evaluate the information they are receiving
- Make decisions about what to do with that information

Using the whole brain

The English language invites us to distinguish feeling from thinking. We accept this invitation whenever we praise people for being *'rational'* and use *'emotional'* as a putdown. Some other languages do not make such a clear distinction. They recognise that **thinking needs feeling** and **feeling needs thinking**.

Recent research by neuroscientists confirms that you cannot isolate the parts of the brain concerned with feeling from those concerned with thinking; they depend upon one another.

Emotional literacy is about ensuring that we really do use our:

Keeping the bridge open

Imagine the emotional brain and the thinking brain as two parts of a town divided by a bridge. To use the whole brain, there has to be continuous passage across that bridge – feelings sparking thoughts, thoughts influencing feelings.

Strong feelings – confusion, anxiety, anger, longing, joy, excitement – tend to overwhelm us, making it more difficult for us to think clearly. If we are flooded by such feelings for too long, we break the links between our feeling and thinking brains. This stops us thinking about the painful messages we are receiving.

The result is that our feelings are no longer available to guide our thinking, and our thinking has little influence over our feeling. When the passage between the thinking brain and the feeling brain is repeatedly blocked, the bridge starts to decay, making it much harder to get from one part of the town to the other.

Emotional literacy involves rebuilding that bridge. We do that by reducing stress and increasing calm.

Thoughts

Feelings

Why we need our whole brain

Emotions are:

- Very fast
- Shaped by deep memories
- Linked to instinct and intuition

They help us make rapid decisions as we assess people and situations.

Thoughts are:

- Quite slow
- Draw on available memory
- Linked to analysis and reflection

They help us consider and reflect on what our feelings are telling us.

The more we can allow our thoughts and our emotions to feed into one another, the better we become at using the information we have available to shape our decisions and judgements.

Feeling disconnected

Anjali sits at the back of the class and never says a word. She is wrapped up in her anxiety about what might happen if she were to make her views known to the rest of the class.

Peter's restless movements during lessons unsettle everyone around him. They sense the simmering anger that occasionally threatens to explode from him.

Anjali and Peter are both locked in uncomfortable feelings which get in the way of their ability to think clearly. Their problem is that previous events in their lives have caused them to interpret the current classroom situation in ways that make it impossible for them to engage in learning.

How to rebuild the thinking-feeling bridge

To help Anjali and Peter reconnect their thinking to their feeling, you need to help them transform their current feeling states from:

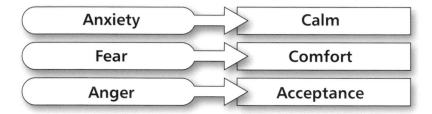

Anxiety	→	Calm
Fear	→	Comfort
Anger	→	Acceptance

This is about helping them to see that school is not like the situation that led to the development of their anxious, fearful and angry responses. They need to experience school as being safe. That means helping them change the stories they are telling themselves about what is happening, or might be about to happen, to them in the classroom.

Stories to help us think

The current stories that Peter and Anjali tell about themselves are unhelpful to learning. They need to evolve other stories that will be helpful.

Thinking – unhelpful	Thinking – helpful
'I don't think people have any real idea of who I am or what I can do.'	*'I know that people value me for what I contribute to whatever we are doing.'*
'I sense that people are just looking out for ways to show me up.'	*'I feel pretty comfortable in most situations.'*
'I wish I was someone else.'	*'I'm okay being me.'*
'It doesn't matter how I say it, my message just doesn't seem to get through.'	*'I feel that people understand what I am saying most of the time, and it sometimes leads to things happening differently.'*
'I just don't seem to be able to do anything that makes a difference.'	*'Whatever challenge I am confronted with, I will find a way to meet it eventually.'*

Shaping a CLASI classroom

You are more likely to help Peter and Anjali evolve a helpful story if they experience an emotional environment in your classroom that makes them – and *everyone* else – feel increasingly **C L A S I**, ie:

Capable — People around me are genuinely interested in enabling me to realise my potential.

Listened to — I am free to say what I think or feel and it may lead to things changing.

Accepted — I can explore different ways of being myself.

Safe — I do not have to hide the way emotions influence what I think, say and do.

Included — I am valued for the distinctive role I play in this class and school.

The importance of these five factors was demonstrated through five years of research* by Antidote into what facilitates emotional literacy in schools.

The stories on the following pages all feature real young people in real schools who have found themselves in a CLASI classroom environment.

*Pastoral Care in Education 23 (4), 5-16. Published by Blackwell on behalf of NAPCE.

The importance of feeling **C**apable

Story 1

Year 9 student Sally is about to have a one-to-one interview with her tutor. Since the tutor regularly tells Sally off for not working hard enough, she is expecting more of the same.

This session, though, is different. It takes place in the deputy head's office. Juice and biscuits have been laid on. The conversation starts slowly. But Sally starts to relax as she begins noticing her tutor's interest in her hobbies and other activities. She can feel herself becoming less stressed by the minute.

The tutor asks Sally to think about what she wants to achieve this year in school, and how she thinks she might achieve it. For the first time in ages Sally starts to see herself as a person rather than just a future GCSE statistic. She has some new ideas about how to choose her GCSE options and she talks enthusiastically about the college courses she might aim for.

When their time together is over, Sally emerges with a genuine belief that her tutor wants the best for her and will do what she can to help her succeed.

The importance of being **L**istened to

Story 2

For weeks the Year 5 students have been trying to tell the lunchtime supervisors and their class teacher that they don't feel safe in the school playground but nobody seems able to hear them.

The problem is the quiet garden. Created a few years earlier as a place for quiet contemplation, it has a bench, trees and some sculpture. Staff members cannot imagine there being any problems with an area so delightful.

Several class members draft the piece of paper that goes into the suggestion box for that week's circle time. Fortunately, the teacher takes their request seriously and after the initial game, two girls explain the problem. Some of the Year 6 boys are taking advantage of the garden's seclusion, and the lack of adult supervision, to beat up members of Year 5 who annoy them.

Once the topic is out in the open, everyone has something to say and the teacher really listens. She goes on to set up an assembly about respecting different parts of the playground, particularly the quiet garden. It is agreed that a lunchtime supervisor will be in or around the area from then on.

The importance of being **A**ccepted

Story 3

Philip is a withdrawn student who seems to live almost entirely in his own world, daydreaming his way through school, apparently uninterested in learning. He isn't picked on and he isn't bullied. He just doesn't appear on anyone's radar.

One day he gets into a conversation with one of his teachers about a lesson on tropical rainforests and the creatures that live in them. When Philip mentions that his hobby is breeding rare spiders and stick insects, the teacher takes a real interest. She asks if she can see the spiders.

The visit that the teacher makes to Philip's home is a breakthrough. She discovers that this quiet and somewhat withdrawn student breeds red-kneed tarantulas, grows bonsai plants and attends world symposia on stick insects in his holidays.

These discoveries made it possible for the school to understand Philip in a new way. It now knows how to foster his skills and help him to achieve.

The importance of being **S** afe

Story 4

Calvin is in year 6. He repeatedly tells people that he doesn't like school and that nobody understands him. His behaviour goes from bad to worse: he calls out in class, is rude and disagreeable with his peers and won't co-operate with teachers. His cockily arrogant exterior hides a lot of inner misery.

It is only when Calvin's dad comes into school one parents' evening to talk to his class teacher that the reasons for his behaviour become clear. Calvin's mum is seriously ill and his dad, a long-haul lorry driver, has to be away a lot of the time.

The result is that Calvin arrives at school having made breakfast for himself, his little sister and his mum. He has been to the corner shop for bread and milk, and has made sandwiches for all three of them.

Once the school recognises the stress upon Calvin, and provides him with a safe place to talk about his feelings, he is able to start engaging with his teacher and co-operating with systems that support him in improving his behaviour. Finally, he can start to learn.

The importance of being **I**ncluded

Story 5

It's touch and go whether Corinne will avoid permanent exclusion. Clearly someone who doesn't like being told what to do, she tends to be disrespectful to teachers. They are continually picking on her for not doing her homework and trying to evade the uniform code with fishnet tights and large jewellery. Nor does she endear herself to staff by the capacity she has to distract other students from their learning.

One day, she auditions for the school play and lands herself a major part. She needs to work really hard and to collaborate with the teachers responsible for costume, stage direction and production. She starts to see these teachers in a new light, and the feeling is mutual. Corinne has a lot of good ideas about how to improve the set. The backdrops are changed to incorporate her suggestions.

The experience of being 'centre stage' does not increase Corinne's arrogance; rather, it starts to soften her attitude towards authority in the school. The relationships with staff and students that she develops continue after the production is over. She wants to work and do well.

Unintended consequences

It is worth remembering that sometimes there are factors outside your control that will limit your capacity to shape a C L A S I experience for your students. The scenario below is repeated all over the country between February and May:

> *GCSEs are approaching and the school has organised a carefully-designed programme to prepare Year 11 for exams. About 40% of them happily apply themselves to the revision that's been set; the rest just don't seem to be able to stop 'messing around'.*
>
> *Once a week the head gives a talk exhorting Year 11 to get on with their work. He tells them their grades aren't only important for their own prospects in life, but also for the school. It's been climbing the league tables and he wants it to climb higher.*
>
> *The head denies it, but staff can see that behaviour gets even worse after his talk.*

It's not difficult to see what's happening. Those students who are not expected to do particularly well are already worried that the exams will mark them down for a lifetime of failure. Every time the headteacher stands up, he triggers in them an acute state of panic. Overwhelmed by these feelings, they become unable to think or to behave in a way that is other than disruptive.

Emotions for learning – bringing it together

This first section has explored the ways in which the emotional experience of children and young people affects how they behave in classrooms.

Anjali and Peter represent what might really be going on for some of the students who sit in front of us each day, students whose experience of school does not lead to them feeling **C**apable, **L**istened to, **A**ccepted, **S**afe and **I**ncluded. The stories on pages 21-25 illustrate how, as teachers, we can respond in ways that support the growth and learning of our students.

The next three sections of the book look at how we can shape classrooms where thinking and feeling work together to facilitate learning. If we want students to feel CLASI, we need to ensure that we **communicate** and **organise** our classrooms so as to breed trusting **relationships**. (See diagram overleaf.)

Looking after the CORE

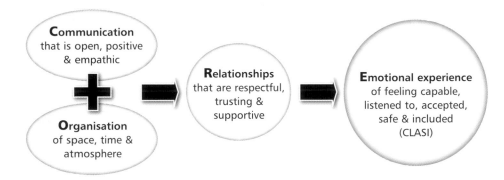

Relationships that Support Learning

The importance of relationships

'The economy, stupid' was a slogan coined during Bill Clinton's 1996 presidential campaign to keep his team on message. *'Relationships, stupid'* needs to be at the heart of your campaign to shape an ever more emotionally literate classroom.

You are an important person in the lives of your students, just by the fact that you are an adult who has authority over them. The more you can communicate that you are interested in knowing them and in them knowing you, the greater the likelihood that you will shape a harmonious classroom community.

When students feel understood and listened to by you, they will find it much easier to understand and listen to each other.

Relationships for learning

Relationships are important for several reasons. Within them, we discover that:

- We are not alone
- Someone will pick us up if we fall or fail; so it is safe to take risks and engage with new, potentially challenging information
- There will be someone to celebrate with if we succeed

Discovering these three things is vital for healthy growth and social functioning. It also helps to reduce the stress of learning in a situation where you constantly have to risk failing and being shown up in a class of around 30 other students.

When you build relationships with students, you provide them with the support and encouragement they need to take the risk of mastering something difficult, whether that be long division, the application of Ohm's law or doing cartwheels.

Student relationships

It is not the prospect of studying that gets most students into school in the morning. They come, instead, to meet people, socialise and discover how to get the most out of being together. In their eyes, any learning that happens is a happy by-product of hanging out together.

Students divide their peers into two groups:

❶ Friends – the people they know, like, go around with and identify with.
❷ Everybody else.

Friendship groups are created by history and culture as well as personal rapport. It's important to help students see that those who are not their friends are nevertheless people who *could* be their friends.

Ensuring that they talk together and work together enables them to discover that they too have things in common. Students are then more likely to learn together and live together in a happy and supportive classroom community.

Why relationships trip us up

But relationships are not straightforward. You and your pupil have particular expectations of each other. You each bring to the classroom ways of thinking and acting that you have learned from your relationships with others. You also bring the messages received during your childhood and beyond. The classroom interaction evolves as a dance between your different expectations of each other.

A girl who has been treated badly by adults in her home life may expect all other adults to treat her the same way. As a well-intentioned teacher, you may be baffled by her constant prickly defensiveness.

A boy who never knew his father may convey great neediness to you, a teacher who shows him kindness. You might be unprepared for the demands that then ensue.

Similarly, if you are looking for emotional warmth that is missing elsewhere in your life, your students will find you intrusive. The most unsettling emotional outbursts in the classroom (or anywhere else, for that matter) result from the discovery by one person that the other is not willing to play the role ascribed to him or her.

Setting boundaries

The complexity of relationships leads some teachers to suggest that they have no place in the classroom:

> *'All we need is a disciplined environment where the students do as they are told and I am free to teach.'*

But the process of teaching and learning is not dry and devoid of feeling. It inevitably involves a complex set of interactions between people. Those interactions trigger a steady flow of emotions.

Our challenge as teachers is to ensure that these emotions facilitate rather than inhibit learning.

That means keeping the relationship dance going while at the same time maintaining firm boundaries.

Setting boundaries

You can maintain that balance by:

- Being aware of where your professional boundaries lie
- Having a repertoire of relational skills
- Noticing when more is being asked of you than is appropriate in your professional role
- Articulating the limits clearly and sympathetically to your students

When teachers and other adults set clear boundaries for classroom relationships, children and young people feel safe enough to let down their defences and engage with others in a way that promotes learning.

Building relationships with R time

Relationships outside natural friendship will not just happen by putting children and young people into the same room together. Teachers need space and permission to establish and sustain the kind of relationships that support learning.

Headteacher Greg Sampson developed 'R time' to help students get to know each other and learn to help each other. The process involves a series of weekly sessions, lasting 10 to 15 minutes, that go like this:

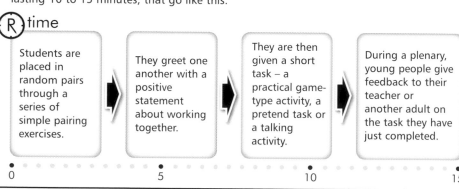

Ⓡ time

| Students are placed in random pairs through a series of simple pairing exercises. | They greet one another with a positive statement about working together. | They are then given a short task – a practical game-type activity, a pretend task or a talking activity. | During a plenary, young people give feedback to their teacher or another adult on the task they have just completed. |

0   5   10   15

Confident to learn with others

In schools learning is often something that people do on their own. Students listen to the teacher, read a book and write quietly at their desks. In the adult world the majority of learning comes through conversation, argument and group discussion.

The richest learning experiences probably involve a mixture of individual study and opportunities to engage with other people's ideas, perspectives and experiences. We need greater self-confidence to work with others than on our own because we have to be able to risk exposing the things we don't understand and can't do to the scrutiny of others. If we can get over that hurdle, the support and encouragement we receive from others will build our resilience and stimulate our creativity.

In our classrooms, there will be **resilient learners** and **fragile learners**. The resilient have learned to draw on the support of others and are robust in facing setbacks and difficulties. Fragile students may achieve well, but will isolate themselves from others. They cannot cope with significant challenges or the experience of failure.

Relationships – bringing it all together

So far we've looked at how emotional literacy in the classroom is about creating more **C L A S I** emotional experiences and shown that it's the quality of relationships that determines the level of CLASI-ness in a classroom or school.

The next section looks at the sorts of classroom conversations that build relationships that support learning.

Open Conversations

The importance of communication

Relationships are shaped through the communications that students receive from their peers, friends and the adults around them. Through conversations, students learn about themselves and about each other. In the process, they learn more about what makes it possible for them to learn most effectively.

Relationships that enable students to feel CLASI are more likely to arise when communication is:

Open communication

> 'Quite often when I am set a task at school, I feel under pressure – perhaps I'm afraid of failing and looking a fool, of being uncool in front of the class. It's really a fear of what other people will think of me. When that kicks in, I just can't think straight.' George, Year 8

George is not alone. Much communication in school is designed to get people doing things they may not be particularly interested in, or confident about, doing. Pressure is applied as a way of stimulating action.

But the stress this creates can make learning more difficult, even impossible.

As teachers, if we want people to become effective learners, we need to combine **directive** communication that tells people what to do, with **open** communication that involves a real interaction between speaker and listener.

Directive Communication +
Open Communication
―――――――――
Effective Teaching
and Learning

Positive communication

When students come into the classroom, they want to hear that you are pleased to see them because of who they are and what they might contribute. That applies whether they arrive smiling, scowling or busily occupied with texting and iPods.

The American psychologist Martin Seligman says that we would all achieve more if we could increase our awareness of the strengths that we possess, and spend less time trying to correct our weaknesses. He has identified 24 character strengths:

Courage
bravery, persistence, integrity, vitality

Wisdom and knowledge
creativity, curiosity, open-mindedness, love of learning, perspective

Justice
responsibility, fairness, leadership

Humanity
love, kindness, social intelligence

Temperance
forgiveness, humility, prudence, self-control

Transcendence
appreciation of beauty, gratitude, hope, humour, spirituality

Noticing and verbally appreciating character strengths is a form of communication that creates a positive emotional environment. This sets the stage for more open conversations.

Empathic communication

Empathy is a quality that enables people to:

- Accept others for who they are
- Experience situations from their perspective
- Communicate in a way that makes sense to the person listening
- Engage constructively in carrying out tasks

Students respond well if you show them that you are interested in their lives and have a sense of what makes them tick. To be empathic with someone, you need to create a mental model of how they think. This can then grow through your experience of them.

Empathic communication

Too often, all you have time to do as a teacher is to build a rough mental model of the whole class. *'They're bright.'* *'They're a handful.'* *'They're really slow.'*

To deepen your empathy, you need to find opportunities to talk to your students as individuals. You can make a start by using time at the beginning and end of lessons to reveal what you have noticed.

'Like the hairdo.'

'That was a great comment you made.'

'You're looking smart today.'

'I liked the way you listened in the lesson.'

Open conversations

Open conversations enable students to build understanding about what is happening emotionally for them and for others. Closed conversations, on the other hand, involve scoring points, presenting counter arguments or otherwise seeking to show how clever you are.

Conversations are open when those who participate in them:

- Take a **genuine interest** in the thoughts and feelings of each other
- Express through what they say and do a **desire to understand better** what the other person is saying

Such open conversations make it possible for young people to explore:

- Assumptions about the way other people think and feel
- Interpretations of other people's actions
- The different ways in which other people see things
- Alternative ways of going about things

Planning for open conversations

You can encourage your students to engage in open conversations when they are:

- Reviewing a learning strategy or experience
- Looking for solutions to a problem
- Planning an event
- Setting individual or class goals
- Considering an emotional issue such as friendship or loss

Doing so will help them:

- Make sense of things that might otherwise be baffling
- Understand what makes each other tick
- Stimulate creative thinking about how they can learn
- Build stronger relationships
- Increase the strategies available for learning and problem-solving

Talking about feelings

Students can only talk about their feelings when the conversation is open. Encouraging children to talk about what they are feeling when they are learning together will help them to manage those feelings better. It is reassuring, for example, for an individual to discover that they are not the only one who gets stressed when doing a test, or feels frustrated about being unable to solve a maths problem.

Talking about their emotional experience helps students to:

- Recognise and put a name to particular feelings
- Anticipate situations and events that will trigger those feelings
- Share with others the difficult feelings they experience
- Learn new approaches to managing those feelings
- Discover how others are affected by external pressures such as parental expectations, predicted test scores and the messages they have received about their abilities

The art of promoting open conversations

You can help your students engage in open conversations by laying aside the role of 'expert' and becoming a 'co-explorer'. (You may find this a bit scary if you're someone who likes to feel in control and has planned every step of a lesson.)

As an expert, you communicate that you *do* know, or that there is something they *ought* to feel. As a co-explorer you need to:

- Show signs of being interested in whatever they are saying
- Use questions that follow the thoughts of the person you are listening to
- Avoid giving answers or reaching conclusions
- Support the speaker in finding ways to express his or her ideas
- Give non-verbal indications that you accept what is being said
- Use reflection to encourage more conversation

These are all elements of **active listening**. Active listening encompasses a wide range of listening skills. (See pages 49-52.)

Active listening

Active listening is the art of listening in a way that **involves** you in the other person's subject matter, rather than passively taking in the other person's words. Listening in an active way communicates that you respect the person who is speaking and value his or her opinion. That helps them to relax and to communicate in a fuller and more coherent way. To listen actively, you need to:

1. Put your own needs to one side.
2. Come alongside the other person.
3. Try to see things through their eyes.

Listening takes time, attention and patience. You need to be aware of your own thoughts and feelings so that you can prevent them getting in the way of your hearing what people are saying to you.

Listening also takes courage. You may hear things that are uncomfortable or distressing. You may want to solve the problem or find a solution. Yet often the most useful thing you can do is just listen.

Making time for active listening

Time for active listening is not readily available during curriculum time, so it helps if you can let students know:

- When you will be available to listen
- How much time you can give

Some secondary teachers agree to have their coffee or their lunch in their classroom one break-time a week. Students then know that the teacher is available for open conversations during that time.

In primary classrooms, teachers sometimes put aside five minutes during class time while students are occupied with a task. They make sure that each child is allocated special talk time once a week or fortnight.

Skills of active listening

The skills involved in active listening include:

Attending
- Eye contact
- Forward body position
- Warm gestures
- Positive facial expressions

Responding
- Repeating words
- Paraphrasing
- Reflecting feelings behind words

Encouraging
- 'Really?'
- 'Tell me more about......'

Clarifying
- 'Do you mean......?'
- 'Can you help me to understand?'

Summarising
- 'As I see it, the situation is......'

Building on other people's ideas
- 'Yes, and......'

An active listening activity

All of us, adults and children alike, need active listening skills. The activity below is one that can help enhance those skills:

1 Divide students into pairs (or threes). One student describes an exciting or frightening incident. The listener pays no attention and offers no eye contact. He or she is restless and repeatedly looks away.

2 Repeat the activity. This time the listener gives *complete* attention.

3 Next, swap roles so that each participant gets to be both a listener and a narrator.

4 Students then discuss the different ways in which they showed they were or were not listening. They discuss the feelings of the narrator and then of the listener.

The experiential nature of this activity means that it raises feelings for all those who take part. Reflecting on those feelings helps young people to notice the impact they have on others when they choose not to listen and highlights ways they can improve their listening skills.

Fostering curiosity

You cannot have open conversations without **curiosity.** Curiosity is the engine of learning. If a young person is interested in something, they will be motivated to learn more. You foster curiosity when you show that you are yourself inquisitive, eg by:

- Valuing and encouraging questions
- Showing as much interest in asking good questions as in reaching right answers
- Giving students space for their own thoughts, ideas and concerns

You also promote curiosity by showing interest in each child or young person as a learner. The child who knows you are keen to understand why he/she finds it difficult to learn is more likely to talk to you about it than the child who continuously hears you asserting how important it is to learn.

Curiosity can only be released in a caring environment where a child feels able to say: *'I can take risks'; 'I can feel vulnerable'; 'I can plunge into uncertainty'.*

When your curiosity is tested

If curiosity is so important, then we need to stimulate it in classrooms. Yet nothing is more likely to undermine our capacity to be curious than disruptive behaviour in the classroom, corridor or playground. Behaviour management techniques teach us to address poor behaviour through systems of sanctions and rewards. But we also need to be able to ask *'what is really going on here?'*. That means trying to:

- Reframe the behaviour by engaging with the possibility that the anger and defiance on display are a normal part of growing up

- Ask whether the behaviour is a sign that something is going on about which you need to find out more

- Recognise that the behaviours we want in school may not be those which the student has learned at home

Only when you show young people that you are interested in why they do what they do can you help them develop more constructive ways of expressing their anger, fear and aggression.

A restorative approach

The traditional response to conflict between students asks:

- What happened?
- Who is to blame?
- What is the appropriate punishment for those at fault?

Restorative approaches, by contrast, use open conversations to work out difficulties that occur between people. A restorative approach asks:

- What perspectives do people have on what has happened?
- Who has been affected and how?
- How can the harm be repaired?
- How can we learn from the situation to do things differently next time?

The aim is to move forward in a way that not only repairs the harm, but also improves relationships in the classroom.

Building resilience

Learning involves setbacks and challenges. Setbacks can easily lead us to change a helpful story (*I can do this*) into an unhelpful one (*I am not good*). The unhelpful story will prevent us from engaging in open conversations.

We need to be resilient enough to accept that setbacks are inevitable and that challenges can be dealt with if we persevere. To become more resilient, you need to know that:

It is okay to make mistakes and fail

Speed is not a virtue

Steady effort solves problems

If students (and adults) are to become robust enough to see failure, struggle, confusion and frustration as part of a normal learning process, they need to hear that someone:

- Believes they can succeed
- Will stay with them through their efforts
- Will not step in *unless* they are asked for help

The value of silence

Open conversations do not necessarily involve endless amounts of talking. Silence is an important part of any conversation: it helps us to listen; it gives us time to think, to reflect on what we have heard and what is being said to us. Silence allows the mind to focus and relax. A relaxed mind can let through information from our feelings that will not otherwise penetrate the hubbub of conversation.

'I felt a little bit angry then. What was that about?'

'Why did what she said then make me feel sad?'

Given a few minutes to think in silence, students can rid themselves of the mental clutter they have picked up during the rest of the day.

Silence is not a regular part of most classroom practice; yet many teachers are experimenting with times of silence during the working day. Some are introducing meditative breathing accompanied by visualisations to help promote calm at various points in the day. (See Antidote's *Emotional Literacy Handbook: promoting whole-school strategies.*)

Communication – bringing it all together

This section has looked at how open communication is essential for encouraging CLASI conversations – the kind that support learning – in classrooms.

Open conversations depend on:

Active listening

Sustaining curiosity

Resolving conflict

Building resilience

Sometimes, however, basic things (eg how space is organised and how well the heating works) can get in the way of your capacity to shape a CLASI environment. The next section covers four essentials:

1 The question of time
2 The teacher's role
3 Organising the learning
4 Fostering a spirit of equality

Classroom Organisation

The time challenge

By now, you may be wondering just how much of a clue the authors of this Pocketbook have about the pressures on today's teachers!

> *'We have to prepare lessons, mark work, attend meetings, run after-school clubs...... We don't have time to talk with all our students about their interests; all that went out with the National Curriculum......'*

But think about it this way: do you ever have to spend time trying to:

- Tackle disruption
- Motivate unengaged students
- Deal with distress caused by classroom quarrels?

Time spent on setting the scene for positive, empathic and open conversations will improve relationships and so ultimately save you time. The time, space and permission that you as a class teacher give to communication are essential ingredients for building relationships that will support learning.

Time and goals

Perhaps time can be better managed if we think differently about our goals. We live in an educational climate that is fixed on objectives and outcomes. Yet having pre-defined outcomes can dismiss all other learning as irrelevant. The problem is exacerbated if the outcomes begin to dominate what is happening in our classrooms. The message we communicate is:

> *Your idea of what you need to learn is not of interest. You've just got to get on and do what you've been told to do.*

The targets, goals and outcomes are unlikely to go away. So, we need to trust that if we start from what young people are curious about, and give them the best possible opportunity to build on that curiosity, they will learn what they need to know. To do that, we have to believe that children and young people really do want to learn. They don't have to be driven towards it. That means saying:

> *We think you are good judges of what you need to know and how you can learn it. We trust that, if you are given the time to engage in conversations with adults and fellow students about what you see, experience and think, then you will learn what you need to know.*

The teacher's role

Alison King, an American professor, once drew a distinction between teachers who were *'sages on the stage'* and those who were *'guides on the side'*.

Sages:

- Know what has to be learned
- Control emotional expressions in class
- Generate the questions for students
- Determine which answers are right

When you are the *'sage on the stage'* you will dominate the classroom. Communication will be addressed to you and you will act as mediator of interaction. You have the knowledge and your job is to impart it.

The teacher's role

When you act as *'guide on the side'*, you see your role as being to help students cope with uncertainty and the anxiety that accompanies not knowing. You facilitate the development of young people's ideas by helping them to build on each other's thoughts and pull things back when you feel the discussion is going off track.

Guides:

* Open things up with questions
* Encourage alternative questions
* Structure the dialogue
* Are open to new learning

Centre stage or in the wings?

Hazel stands at the centre of the class and asks two students to give out exercise books as the others file in. She calls for quiet: 'Listen or you won't know what to do.' The focus is on her. Students wait for her instructions.

In another classroom down the corridor, students come into the room, read the instructions that are already written on the board, pick up their exercise books and settle down to work on a short, introductory task. Only when the last student has arrived and everyone is engaged in thinking about the problem that has been posed does George speak to the whole group.

The second teacher is much less prominent, but just as much in charge. He greets students, makes contact at the door. He has a set of expectations and anticipates that students will adhere to them. He has more time to communicate his pleasure at seeing his class. He speaks to one or two students at a time in a quiet voice, encouraging them to settle down and get on with the task.

At the centre of the second classroom lies the student and his or her learning. The teacher has moved away from centre stage into a supporting and facilitative role.

Organising the learning through ritual

A ritual is a set of actions that are performed for their symbolic value. Rituals can happen at regular intervals, on specific occasions, or as agreed by the class to change the mood or signal an event such as the beginning of circle time, going to assembly or tidying up the classroom before the end of a lesson or story.

Mrs Ritchey always plays a special piece of music to signal the beginning of circle time. When the children hear the music, they move the tables and take their chairs to form a circle. They aim to have the circle ready before the music comes to an end so that they are sitting quietly listening as it ends and circle time can begin.

In the nearby secondary school, meanwhile, Mr Gale uses the Countdown music to signal packing up time at the end of a lesson.

Rituals

Classroom rituals help create a sense of students being in control. The ritual signals the need for them to manage their own learning by changing pace, activity or location in the classroom.

Because rituals are predictable, they reduce stress. They are important because they:

- Build community by bringing the whole school together around the same event
- Provide a change of pace in the school day, week or year
- Provide a focal point for more open conversations and relationship building

Organising the learning using enquiry

Rituals provide structural markers to the learning by breaking up activities or periods of time, but there are many other ways of organising the learning.

One useful organising approach is Philosophy for Children (P4C), a form of enquiry that provides students with opportunities to explore questions as a community of learners. It requires students to use the skills of active listening and to link emotional responses with intellectual enquiry while exploring a question that interests the class.

An enquiry is a whole-class activity that involves everyone sitting in a circle as they share their views and argue their points.

The diagram on the next page summarises the different phases of an enquiry.

Philosophical enquiry

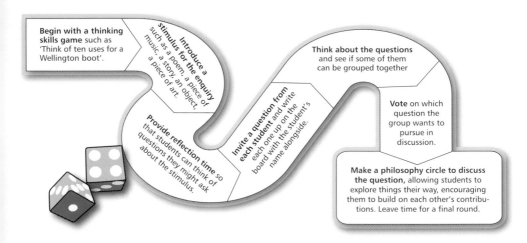

Begin with a thinking skills game such as 'Think of ten uses for a Wellington boot'.

Introduce a stimulus for the enquiry such as a poem, a piece of music, a story, an object, a piece of art.

Provide reflection time so that students can think of questions they might ask about the stimulus.

Invite a question from each student and write each one up on the board with the student's name alongside.

Think about the questions and see if some of them can be grouped together

Vote on which question the group wants to pursue in discussion.

Make a philosophy circle to discuss the question, allowing students to explore things their way, encouraging them to build on each other's contributions. Leave time for a final round.

Fostering a spirit of equality

A P4C enquiry is a truly open conversation hosted, but not dominated, by the teacher. It fosters a spirit of equality in the classroom where the teacher's view or knowledge does not take a higher place than the children's.

A philosophical enquiry frees students from pre-set curriculum outcomes and the obligation to say the 'right' thing. They become self-managed and self-directed learners. They develop:

Problem-solving skills

Reasoning

Empathy

Persuasion

Oral fluency

They also become more concerned for the common good: they want to resolve conflicts, work together and have the courage to defend their point of view.

Time and space for joy and flow

It is said that when Aristotle taught at the Academy in 4thC Athens, he'd stand outside the classroom doors. If he didn't hear laughter within a short period of time, he'd go in to find out why the students weren't learning. Students often assume that if they're having fun they're not learning. Some adults think the same.

> Joy increases our capacity to learn and our ability to persist with difficult tasks.

Psychologist Mihaly Csikszentmihalyi says that people are at their happiest when they are in a state of *'flow'*, fully immersed in what they are doing and experiencing feelings of freedom, enjoyment, fulfilment and skill. Such learning is a joyful and absorbing activity. To create *'flow'* you need to ensure there is:

- A balance between the challenge of the activity and the skill of the learner
- Enough time for focused attention to develop

The more we help young people to access an intrinsic desire to learn, the more likely they are to develop resilience and curiosity.

Introduction

 Emotions and Learning

 Relationships that Support Learning

 Open Conversations

 Classroom Organisation

 Classroom Communities ◀

 Telling Better Stories

 Emotional Literacy in the Staffroom

Classroom Communities

From individuals to cohesive community

A class is a community of young people drawn from the wider school community.

When you put young people at their desks, facing the front for teacher-centred instruction, you are shaping a **regimented** community.

When you group them around tables to facilitate conversation and group learning, you are trying to create a **collaborative** community.

If your students use the opportunity to get on each other's nerves, you will end up with a **warring** community.

In working to shape more emotionally literate classrooms, we want to help students become increasingly collaborative. We need to know how to help them work in groups. This section looks at how groups are formed, evolve and operate and how we can use circle time and groupwork to take a class from a disparate set of individuals to a cohesive community of people who know one another and support one another's learning.

Why groups are so important

Our most basic human needs are for **connection & relationship** and **autonomy & individuation**

We cannot satisfy one of these needs unless we can also satisfy the other.

We need strong relationships if we are to develop our individuality, but at the same time our capacity to be autonomous enables us to build stronger relationships. When we cannot satisfy both needs, we become anxious and insecure. We try to cope with this anxiety through submissive or aggressive patterns of behaviour.

In groups we can increase our connectedness to others which will in turn enable us to become more autonomous.

Connection & relationship

Autonomy & individuation

Groups don't happen on their own

Groups provide opportunities not only to learn to work collaboratively but also to:

- Get to know and respect each other
- Discover and value each other's differences
- Engage *actively* in their learning
- Develop higher-level thinking

This sounds good. However, putting people into groups doesn't mean they will necessarily work *as* groups. It's quite possible for students to use groups as an opportunity to:

- Have a rest while other people do the work
- Show off and get everyone's attention
- Retreat into invisibility

To ensure there's more of the first and less of the second, we need to work out how to set up and develop our classroom groups so they really work.

Circle time

Circle time has traditionally been seen as a primary school approach to creating cohesive communities of learning. In recent years, though, more and more secondary schools have seen how circle time can contribute to teaching and learning.*

It involves doing groupwork in a circle and it's important that all children feel included. It opens up opportunities for young people to express what they are feeling and to discover more about who they are through their interactions with each other.

The diagram on the next page shows a common structure for circle time:

Recommended authors writing about circle time in primary and secondary schools include: Barbara Maines & George Robinson, Jenny Mosley, Tina Rae, Sue Roffey.

CORNWALL COLLEGE
LEARNING CENTRE

Circle time

 Circle time

| A game allows people to connect emotionally through having a bit of fun. | A round gives everyone an opportunity to introduce themselves and find their voice. | An activity focuses people's attention on a topic or issue. | A conference explores what people learned through carrying out the activity. | An ending ritual brings the group process to a close and puts the difficult issues back in their boxes. |

When to use circle time

In primary classrooms, circle time is often a timetabled, weekly event. It provides an opportunity for the class to engage in speaking and listening while having some fun together.

Sometimes, teachers use this time for structured curriculum content. At other times, the time and space are provided for the children's agenda, including the discussion issues that have arisen in the class during the week.

Secondary schools that have adopted circle time use it in tutorial time or as an approach for teaching PSHE. The content is often prescribed. The circle approach enables students to engage with the subject under discussion at a personal level, examining their attitudes, values, opinions and beliefs so that they can make informed decisions about their lives.

Shaping effective groups

Groups work when the people in them:

- Listen to what other people are saying
- Allow people to say whatever they are thinking or feeling
- Take responsibility for their own contributions
- See their role as being to help others contribute
- Can agree how they will make decisions
- Have ways of resolving their conflicts

You can help shape more effective groups by talking with your students about:

- What enables them to feel safe in a group
- The roles they play in groups
- The stages that groups go through
- How they make decisions

Group size

You need different sized groups for different tasks.

If students are going to explore their personal opinions around a topic that some may find uncomfortable, they need to be given the chance to choose who they work with in a **small group.** This may also be a good idea when students have only just started working in groups.

If a discussion has implications for the whole class, eg you are talking about taking an assembly or going on a trip, then everybody needs to gather in a **large group.**

A small group may lack sufficient resources, expertise and diversity of ideas to create a rich group discussion. The large group is more intimidating for some students and doesn't anyway provide sufficient opportunity for everyone to have a say. It's likely that some people will become bored, restless or disruptive.

You can start and end the lesson with the **class as a whole**, but break them into **smaller groups in between.**

The needs of a group

In the 1930s, an American psychologist Abraham Maslow was studying monkeys and noted that some needs took priority over others. He developed the idea that we all have a 'hierarchy of needs', certain things have to be taken care of first if we are to realise our potential. We can apply this to groups:

1 Physiological — Group members need to feel physically comfortable before they can engage.

2 Safety — They need to be confident that no one will put them down or make them feel bad.

3 Belonging — They can then start to experience themselves as a valuable part of the group.

4 Esteem — This will enable them to feel good about what they are contributing to the group task.

5 Self-actualising — As a result, they will start to feel more personally fulfilled.

The group life cycle

Much has been written about the stages that groups go through as they form and grow. A common model, based on Bruce Tuckman's 'Developmental Sequence in Small Groups', identifies five stages:

1. Forming
People begin getting to know each other and explore ways of relating.

2. Storming
As communication opens up, conflicts come to the surface. The group starts to feel uncomfortable.

3. Norming
They work out what is expected of them and how they are going to behave with each other.

4. Performing
The group becomes more effective at getting tasks done while looking after everybody's needs.

5. Mourning
The group's task is done and it has to deal with feelings around ending and separating.

Tuckman's original model is linear, but you'll find that there's often cyclical movement in stages 2-4. Other variations occur, but generally speaking, small groups follow a reasonably predictable pattern.

Group composition

In a classroom, work has to be done before you can bring people together to form a group. Different group compositions fit different purposes, eg highly personal and sensitive information may be better discussed in friendship groups; whereas random groups help to mix the class up and to make connections outside immediate friendship groupings.

Types of group composition

- Friendship groups (self-selecting)
- Peer groups (teacher-chosen)
- Random groups
- Single gender groups
- Mixed gender groups
- Mixed age groups
- Learning styles
- Interests
- Personality types
- Intellectual ability

Stage 1 – group forming activities

Forming the group is about enabling group members to get to know one another, and to feel more comfortable by knowing and being known in the group. The activities that follow are useful ice-breakers.

Name games

Use a soft ball or bean bag. Throw it to someone who provides their name. Once the names are known, throw the bean bag and call the name of the recipient.

Self-introductions

People stand in a circle and introduce themselves by giving their name and one of their likes and one dislike. Alternatively, try alliterative names: '*I am cheerful Cheryl*'.

Circle games

A range of good 'warm-up' games such as '*Zoom-Eek*', '*Zip-Zap-Boing*' and '*Cross the Circle*' can be found in circle time books such as *Circles, PSHE and Citizenship. (See page 126.)*

Stage 1 – group forming activities

Interviews

Pairs of students interview one another to find out as much as they can about the other person.

Unfinished sentences

Students sit in a circle and each person has a chance to finish a sentence such as 'I am......' and 'I like......'.

Charades

People act out hobbies or interests for group participants to guess.

Continuum

People stand on a line number from 0 to 10, according to how strongly they agree or disagree with an opinion.

Trust-building exercises

People stand close together. Everyone closes their eyes and reaches out to take hold of a hand. Eyes are opened and the group tries to disentangle the knot without letting go a hand.

Stage 2 – group storming

You know that conflict is bound to happen at some stage during the life of an effective group. But already the students in your class are shouting, being unreasonable, withdrawing in frustration.

Chances are you will conclude that the whole thing is a disaster and you want to close down the group or take it over. You have to keep telling yourself:

- Conflict is a sign that positive things are happening
- People now feel free to express their true views
- Voices other than the dominant ones are being heard
- The result is going to be a richer group experience

It helps students if you have a positive attitude to conflict. Sensing your confidence that conflicts can be worked through, students will become less confrontational.

Stage 3 – group norming

This is the stage when you as teacher *stop:*
* Setting goals
* Asking the questions
* Responding to the answers that come up
* Taking responsibility for keeping the discussion on track
* Pointing out the connections between ideas
* Drawing conclusions from the learning

The group can then start to become increasingly:
* Focused on the task
* Responsible for completing that task
* Creative in how it does the task
* Attentive to getting the best out of group members
* Able to take the credit for its success

At this stage it is useful to think with students about the sorts of skills they need to make an effective group.

Stage 3 – group norming

Key skills for the group are likely to include some of the following:

- Look at the person who is currently speaking
- Don't feel you have to say something just because the silence has lasted a while
- Let the ideas that come to you evolve before you speak them
- Link what you say to what the previous speaker has said
- Try to make other links to what has been said
- Make it clear whether you are agreeing or disagreeing with a speaker
- Look for areas of agreement even when you disagree
- Try not to get people's backs up
- Feel confident that you have something worthwhile to contribute

Stage 4 – group performing

When the storms have subsided and the norms have established, people will need to take up different roles in the group. These will be **task roles** or **maintenance roles**:

Task roles

- Getting the job done
- Keeping a focus on the task
- Identifying and clarifying that task
- Coming up with ideas and possible answers
- Checking on what has been achieved
- Keeping track of time
- Being tough

Maintenance roles

- Looking after people
- Giving the group cohesion
- Making sure everyone is included and has a role to play
- Helping communication in the group
- Negotiating between group members
- Providing warmth
- Giving the appearance of being 'soft'

Stage 4 – group performing

Task roles

The initiator
Starts things off and may be thought
of as the group 'leader'.

The clarifier
Takes people's contributions and teases
out their precise meaning in relation to
the task. Encourages clarity and makes links.

The information giver
Provides information which enables the group to get the task done.

The questioner
Steps back from the immediate to ask questions that tackle assumptions or help to
define the task more clearly.

The summariser
Pulls contributions together to provide a way of checking what has been achieved.

Stage 4 – group performing

Maintenance roles

The supporter
Demonstrates warmth by smiling, eye-contact and head-nodding as well as saying things that make people feel valued.

The joker
Provides light relief, humour and opportunities for the group to release nervous energy. This is done without putting anyone down or expressing ridicule.

The sharer
Provides personal information, relevant to the task, which enables the group to talk with each other as people and relate on a deeper level.

The observer
Notices when the group has become stuck, thinks about what is going on and, through observation, allows the group to acknowledge the emotions getting in the way of progress.

Stage 4 – group performing

Group observer

It may be worth asking one member of a group to act as the observer. This is best done as a transparent activity where the whole class is aware of the roles that people in groups fulfil before the activity begins.

The observer is given a sheet listing the roles you are trying to develop in the group and is asked:
a) to **tick** every time someone fulfils one of the roles and
b) to **write down examples** of the roles or skills being demonstrated.

Towards the end of the lesson, the group is asked to reflect on how well they worked together and to see if they can remember who demonstrated which roles. The observer can then give feedback from the information collected.

It is important that everyone knows they can take on any of the roles in a group and swap roles any time. There isn't one questioner, one summariser etc.

Stage 4 – group performing

Group observer

Name						
Supporter						
Sharer						
Questioner						
Initiator						
Clarifier						
Summariser						
Joker						

Notes:

Stage 5 – group mourning

Any change in the make-up of the group is a form of ending that will be associated with difficult feelings. If the group has bonded well, there will be the pain of separation. If the group has not worked so well, there will be anger and frustration at the missed opportunities.

All endings need to be marked as a time of loss for the group. They are losing the group they were. They must adjust to moving into new groups. You can help manage these feelings by:

- Acknowledging that this group is going to end
- Allowing space for students to express their feelings about this
- Taking time to think back over what they have achieved
- Encouraging them to create a symbolic object to remind them of what they have done together
- Think about how they will use the skills they've developed in their future groups
- Tie up any loose ends

Classroom communities – bringing it all together

In this section we've looked in more detail at helping a class of students to get the most out of being together by giving them opportunities to:

- Appreciate different experiences, attitudes and perspectives
- Experience how to learn from and with each other

The richness of learning in communities comes from the fact that people experience themselves as being in relationships that make it possible for them to feel CLASI. How you organise the classroom and structure communication makes that possible.

The next section looks at how students can further deepen their learning through the way they evolve their individual and collective stories.

Telling Better Stories

The importance of our own stories

The stories we tell about ourselves are the internal mental framework through which we make sense of the world around us and decide how we are going to respond, eg with warmth or anger; curiosity or defensiveness.

A boy who is used to finding his every thought greeted with, *'You don't know what you are talking about'* will tell himself a story about how it is not worth using his mind, because he'll end up feeling stupid one way or another. (Remember Peter and Anjali.)

We help people change by enabling them to tell each other better stories about:

- Where they came from
- Themselves as learners
- Themselves as members of the classroom community
- Where they are going

As a teacher, you are at the centre of a rich matrix of narratives. The more you can use them and work with them, the richer the experience of learning you will provide for your students.

Stories and emotional literacy

Page 19 drew a distinction between stories that are helpful and those that are unhelpful.

How can we enable students to drop the unhelpful stories and adopt helpful ones?

Julie Leoni's doctoral research with disengaged young people (University of Birmingham) showed that what enables people to change their internal story is having the opportunity to make sense of experiences they have found disturbing and distressing. This involves bringing together the facts about what they experienced with the feelings that are associated with them. If this does not happen, they cannot change the patterns of behaviour they developed as a way of surviving what they were going through.

We can change the story we tell ourselves inside and we can also use other people's stories in the form of literature – story-telling and story-writing – as a way of making sense of our internal world.

Storytelling

Reading stories to a class is not just an infant school activity. Stories come in many forms from newspaper articles to poems, from fiction to factual accounts.

Choosing a story to read to your class gives you an opportunity to show them that you understand what they are currently going through. If they are missing a friend who has left the class, you can tell them a story about loss. If they are worrying about something that happened, you can tell them a story about anxiety.

As you tell the story, you can emphasise emotional messages with your tone of voice and physical gestures. The more you can maintain eye contact and observe reactions, the more attention you will receive. This is much easier, of course, if you can *tell* the story rather than read it.

As you describe the emotions experienced by the characters, you will widen the range of feelings that your students can experience and think about. Do not labour the points that you see the story as making. Children and young people can make sense of the story for themselves, as long as you give them the space to reflect and talk about it.

Moving emotional boulders

Difficult feelings can be experienced by young people as horrible, immovable boulders. Stories are the best means you have for moving and removing those boulders.

For this to happen, young people have to:

- Place themselves in the stories they are reading, really empathising with the dilemmas of the central character
- Learn from the story that emotions come from somewhere
- Recognise that stories are about the transformation of feelings through action

Writing stories

It's not just from reading and hearing stories that children develop.
The opportunity to *write* stories builds emotional literacy in a number of ways:

Content
Directs attention to how the writer experiences him- or herself and the world. It explores how events relate to feelings.

Drafting
Builds resilience as the writer works to craft the story so that it communicates his or her experience to others.

Journey
Takes the writer on an emotional journey of frustration, panic and isolation which can be transformed into feelings of excitement, belonging and interest.

Meaning
Helps the writer to discover what is important to him or her and what he or she wishes to communicate with others.

The beauty of metaphor

It is often not appropriate for young people to talk about the difficult feelings they are experiencing. To do so would be to expose too much of themselves. Indeed, the feelings may be too raw even to be thought about.

In discussing a story, though, they can talk about how a *character* felt, rather than how *they* felt.

Andy once asked his students to write an account of their feelings. He was disappointed with what they delivered. He then asked them to write about how it felt to be an old oak tree. The language they used was much richer, and the feelings expressed much deeper. It was clearly easier for his students to process difficult feelings when writing about being a tree.

It is their capacity to provide metaphorical accounts of what individuals – or whole class groups – are experiencing that gives stories such a power to help in the processing of complex feelings.

The class story

Every class, whether primary or secondary, has its *own* story to tell. It is a story of what they have experienced together, the feelings that have been provoked and the stories they tell to explain those feelings. Sometimes the story helps the class to learn; often it does not.

All too often, the story is never told. It is an unarticulated, commonly held set of beliefs that have grown out of the experiences of the group while it has been together. These can have a positive or a negative impact.

Often a group's story will focus around being good or not good, wanted or unwanted, accepted or rejected as a group. They can relate to behaviour such as, *'We're the bad / difficult / good group'*. Or they might relate to successes and defeats in annual activities such as *'the sporty group'*, *'the couch potatoes'*, etc.

The class that didn't matter

Class Story

This particular Year 9 class had a story they told about themselves. It was a story about how they didn't matter and they had been telling it for two years, ever since they had lost their tutor and experienced a succession of supply teachers.

Knowing that they were not worth anything meant there was no point in paying much attention to what happened in lessons. Their teachers experienced them as a pretty recalcitrant and angry bunch of students. Their story gave them an identity – 'the difficult class', 'the impossible class', 'the class that nobody wanted to teach'.

It only took a morning. They worked together on a metaphorical scenario about being trapped on a desert island after their plane had crashed. They saw how good they were at working as a team, at learning from their mistakes. They started to talk with each other about what had happened and the conclusions they had drawn.

By changing the story they told about themselves, they could shift from the class that wasn't interested in learning to the class that wanted to learn.

Building the class story

A class story will affect the way students relate to one another and behave together, but if the story has never been articulated, no one can understand why they behave the way they do. Neither staff nor students can make sense of what is going on. If the class story is positive and affirming, people will feel CLASI and learn well. If, on the other hand, the class story is negative, the emotional experiences will not be CLASI and learning will be impaired.

It is only when a class is given **time, space** and **permission** with someone who affords them **respectful relationships** that they can think and talk about their story. The process of telling the story opens up the possibility of change.

A secondary teacher might like to use tutor time or a PSHE lesson. If there is a specific issue, a class might be taken off timetable for a couple of lessons to work with the tutor and head of year or pastoral manager. In primary schools, circle time can be used as the forum for finding out about the class story.

The next page outlines one way you might like to do it.

Building the class story

1. Arrange the class into groups of 5-6, each with a good balance of active and passive students who feel comfortable with each other. Ask students in their groups to recount the story of anything that's happened since they came to the school. Each tells their story. The group then chooses one story to tell the class.

2. Agree rules on listening/being a good audience, and a protocol for what happens if a story might make someone in the room feel uncomfortable.

3. Each group in turn tells their story and the others listen. (Agree beforehand that the teacher will make a note of the details as part of the record of this process.)

4. Invite general comments on the big themes that arise. Ask the students in their groups to come up with one thing they want to say about the stories they've heard and then to allow you to share what you'd like to say.

You'll find the stories small groups of students tell reflect the overarching themes that make up the class story. These can be further discussed before considering ways of **changing or challenging** them or of **finding alternative stories** which are more helpful to the class.

Bringing it all together

So far in this book we have:

- Explored how to promote emotional literacy by making people feel more **CLASI**
- Considered **CLASI** relationships as a foundation for learning
- Looked at the role of emotional literacy in developing open conversations
- Thought about how to develop cohesive and supportive groups from classes of disparate individuals
- Examined the stories that individuals and groups tell and how to change them to more helpful stories to support learning

Time now to turn our attention to the people who can make all this happen. Without emotional literacy in the staffroom, the quest for emotional literacy in the classroom is a lost cause.

Emotional Literacy in the Staffroom

Emotions in the staffroom

Emotional states are contagious: one person's mood or agitation, excitement or joy will be communicated to the people around them in a way that generates feelings in response. Sometimes emotions are replicated in others; at other times the response is an attempt to moderate or ameliorate the feelings observed. Rarely do people remain unaffected by others' moods and emotions.

In schools:

- Students are affected by what goes on in relationships between staff
- Stress may get dumped in the staffroom, rather than being dealt with there
- Emotional distress is communicated even when people don't talk about the issues that are bothering them
- Stressed individuals are likely to become defensive, aggressive or withdrawn

Adults who are locked in their own emotional states with no place, time or permission to either recognise how they are feeling or talk about it will communicate those feelings to colleagues and students alike.

Staffroom encounter

Staffroom Story 1

Miss Jagdev comes into the staffroom at break. Her face is flushed and she is slightly out of breath. She has just been up against the notorious group in year 8 that makes most members of staff feel they are no longer cut out for a career in teaching.

Head of faculty Mrs Pritchard spots Miss Jagdev but barely registers her flustered state. She calls out that she wants a word. Her tone of voice is sharp and authoritarian.

Before Mrs Pritchard even reaches her, Miss Jagdev is on the defensive. By the time Mrs Pritchard asks her about the reports that were due in yesterday, she is ready for a fight. She has a whole raft of excuses and good reasons why the reports (which are nearly finished anyway) are not already with Mrs Pritchard. The conversation goes from bad to worse as Mrs Pritchard pulls rank and tells her, in an abrupt manner, that she expects the reports in her pigeonhole by 4.00 pm.

The learning support assistant is very surprised to find a usually calm and cheerful Miss Jagdev shouting at her top set Year 10s in the period after break.

In another staffroom

Staffroom Story 2

Down the road, Mr Jones comes into the staffroom in the local primary school bemoaning Carlotta in his current year 4. He finds her a real challenge. She won't stay in her seat, constantly shouts out in class and can't seem to stop interfering with what everyone else in the room is doing.

Mr Jones has had it! His patience is stretched to breaking point and his sense of competence is severely depleted. As he voices his frustration and sense of impotence, Mrs Jenkins comments, 'What? Carlotta? She was fine in my class last year.'

Mr Jones returns to his classroom feeling even less able to deal with Carlotta. Within a few weeks, he is off work with stress.

How aware are you?

The main problem in these two situations is that the teachers are unaware of the effect they are having on the people around them. Possibly they are even unaware of the emotional events taking place inside themselves.

The fast and furious pace of a school day can often mean that frustration, anxiety, anger and disappointment go underground. In some schools, this can be further exacerbated by a staffroom and school culture that insists on everyone speaking positively at all times.

The emotional states may be unrecognised, but they are nonetheless communicated. Sometimes, staff need some reflective time to go back through events, talk about them with a colleague and find more helpful ways of dealing with their own emotions and the interactions they have with other people.

Developing awareness

Self-awareness is the keystone of emotional literacy. It encompasses how well you know yourself and understand the way you think and feel, both as an individual and in a group context. Self-awareness shapes your ability to manage how you:

- Express emotions
- Cope with difficult and uncomfortable feelings
- Increase and enhance positive and pleasant feelings

It will help you to:

- Concentrate better
- Make better relationships
- Behave more appropriately
- Work more productively with those around you

Self-awareness is not just an individual attribute, it's a collective one too. It is helpful for staff groups (such as teaching assistants, teachers, office staff and site staff) to become more aware of the way they work together and the impact they have on one another or on other groups of staff.

Becoming even more self-aware

To become more self-aware, you need to find someone with whom you can have regular conversations about the variety of emotions you experience in your day-to-day life, and how they affect your attitudes and behaviour. Someone who will:

- Listen attentively
- Help you explore
- Be open to sharing his or her anxieties and fears
- Provide positive input and support

> O Wad some power
> the giftie gie us
>
> To see oursels as
> ithers see us!
>
> Robert Burns, *To a Louse*

Clearing the space for a conversation with such a person will allow you to look at things from new angles, so that fresh perspectives can emerge. If things work well, you will at some point find yourself saying, *'I hadn't thought of it that way before.'*

Such a change of perspective is usually enough to reveal new insights into why you are finding particular situations so difficult. From there, it will be much easier to discover solutions.

Looking after yourself

A key reason why people find it hard to respond in ways that make others feel CLASI is because they don't feel CLASI themselves.

As adults, we cannot depend on other people to make us feel good all the time. It is always nice, of course, if they do. But we have to develop ways of talking to ourselves, soothing ourselves and managing ourselves that enable us to keep our sense of balance and proportion. If you want to avoid feeling overwhelmed by the challenges of school life, it helps if you can:

• Find out what triggers your stress levels
• Develop strategies to manage the difficult situations you cannot avoid
• Know what soothes you if you find yourself feeling overwhelmed
• Find a creative outlet to dump whatever is getting to you
• Manage your time well so that you are not always fighting against the clock
• Use positive talk to prepare yourself for events you expect to find challenging
• Try to stop ruminating on less successful experiences
• Treat your body fantastically well

Emotional bank accounts

It is helpful to think about the staffroom as a financial establishment where the currency is emotional well-being. Some people are good at giving themselves currency by noting the things that go well for them. Other people are always cash poor, because they forever focus on the things that go wrong or badly.

Currency withdrawals	Currency deposits
Lessons going badly	A lesson that goes well
A deadline being missed	Pleasant, affirming exchanges
A communication being misunderstood	Positive feedback from a
A situation mishandled	student/parent/colleague

We all need to keep a reasonable level of currency on deposit so that we don't have to steal currency from a colleague's account in order to boost our own. When we have a good, healthy emotional account, we are more resilient to knocks and challenges and we have currency to give away to other people.

How you say it makes a difference

Staffroom Story 3

It's lunchtime at Buxted Primary and Margaret goes to the Ladies to put herself together again. She'd been quietly eating her sandwich and ruminating on the morning's difficult events when her older colleague Kiran had taken it upon herself to tell some 'home truths' about Margaret's classroom management and timekeeping.

The comments that had so successfully pierced Margaret's personal armour and wounded her were partly true, yet also distorted and exaggerated. They were empty of compassion and held no invitation for discussion, conversation or dialogue.

The emotional currency taken by Kiran from Margaret's account has left her feeling totally bankrupt. Her initial response is to withdraw and say 'never again will I make myself vulnerable'.

Margaret might have fared better if she had chosen to:

- Talk to herself in an affirming way and notice the things that have gone right, such as 'I was on time for all my lessons but one today'

- Find a friend to talk to about classroom management issues and so take control over the situations that cause her difficulty

Conditions for reflection

We have said that taking time to reflect with a colleague or friend is a really helpful way of keeping your currency high and ensuring that you have emotional experiences that make you feel CLASI. Reflection also provides opportunities to feel listened to ourselves, which in turn gives us greater capacity to listen to other people, both students and colleagues.

If you are to have a truly reflective conversation with a colleague, or colleagues, you need to ensure that:

- There are no power differences that will make it difficult for you to be open
- You have a stretch of time available that will not be interrupted
- You can use a space that will remain free of intrusion
- You are both/all committed to helping each other hear what is being said
- You will not be judged for the failures and mistakes you want to talk about
- Nothing that you have said will be repeated to someone else without your permission

The shape of a reflective conversation

Experience

Someone describes a situation that they are finding difficult.

Reflection

Others describe what they hear in what has been said and what thoughts it provokes in them.

Outcome

The original contributor reveals what he or she is going to do, or stop doing, as a result of what has been said.

Solve problems with other people

Staffroom Story 4

For weeks, Jane had been feeling exasperated with nine-year-old Dan. She knew he was having a tough time at home after his father's death but she couldn't just ignore his determination to stop everyone else learning by publicly refusing to do what she asked. In honest moments, she admitted to herself that she felt like hitting him.

One afternoon, Jane had the chance to share her experience with some colleagues. *'I've tried everything to get him back on the learning track,'* she said. Then one of her colleagues said something that really struck her: *'Have you thought of the possibility that the feelings you are experiencing are the feelings Dan is experiencing?'*

The following day, Jane was quietly asking Dan to carry out a piece of writing. Perhaps perceiving the change in her tone, he said to her *'I hate you'*. She hesitated for a moment before replying, *'Just because I'm your teacher doesn't mean you have to like me'*. Immediately, Dan started to relax. For the first time, he felt that someone knew what he was going through. He could let go of his anger and begin to engage.

In **CLASI** terms, Jane's conversation with her colleague enabled her to feel more **capable**. Seeing Dan in a new way gave her a new approach which worked.

A professional is also a person

One of the difficulties with emotional literacy at work is that we are expected to be professional people who can behave and respond appropriately at all times. This is not an easy task, particularly as we take our feelings around with us. We do not have one set of feelings at home and another set of feelings at work.

It may not be appropriate for us to tell colleagues that our partner is sick, our marriage is on the rocks, a parent is making us feel guilty or one of our kids is causing serious trouble at their school. But the chances are they will notice that something is up.

We may not want their sympathy, and we certainly are not interested in the advice they long to give us. However, we would like them at least to acknowledge what we are going through and how it is affecting our ability to give of our best.

Getting the balance right between being professionally discreet and personally open is at the heart of how we manage our emotional well-being in the staffroom.

Nothing stays at home

Staffroom Story 5

Isaac had a difficult morning. He turned the key in the ignition but the car wouldn't start. He tried everything he could think of. Nothing! Fortunately, his wife had a car. She could drop him off at school on her way to work.

As he went indoors, he heard his eldest daughter say to her mum, 'Did you buy the ingredients for my cooking lesson today? We're making a flan, I need cheese, eggs, milk and an onion.' His wife exploded with irritation at her daughter's lack of forethought. Isaac realised that asking for a lift was probably not the wisest move as they would now be heading for the supermarket. He decided to walk.

Some 30 minutes later, frozen and weighed down with marking, he arrived at school – late – to find that he had been taken for cover in his only free period. He also had a meeting with a parent straight after school so he wouldn't be able to sort out his car. His tutor group wondered why Mr Okobi was so short-tempered and irritable that day.

Perhaps Isaac would have had better rapport with his class if he had owned how he felt, explained that his anger had nothing to do with the class, and generally provided a model of emotional maturity for his students.

Valuing yourself

A flow of emotional currency communicates the value and respect that we all look for in our relationships. If we don't invest some time in ourselves, we become emotionally poor and protective of our meagre reserves, resulting in difficult and fragile relationships. Value yourself by taking time to:

Be calm and grounded – serenity comes from noticing beauty and enjoying peaceful moments.

Have fun with friends, partners and family – pleasurable experiences and laughter release serotonin and create a surge of well-being.

Stimulate your grey cells with intellectual pursuits – being a learner who enjoys study, reading and debate communicates to your students that learning is lifelong.

Attend to diet, exercise, relaxation and work/life balance – pay attention to the balance of your life to avoid become burnt out and exhausted. Holidays must not be the only times that you find for recuperation.

Appendix

The ten principles of emotional literacy

Principle	Don't	Do
1. Focus on feelings	**Don't** become preoccupied with *what* people are doing.	**Do** think about *why* they are doing what they are doing, and what feelings may cause them to act in that way.
2. Maintain curiosity	**Don't** assume that you know what is going on.	**Do** keep asking yourself what is *really* going on.
3. Spot the story	**Don't** think of any incident in isolation from what you know.	**Do** use all the information available to work out the story behind what someone is saying or doing.
4. Look after the physical environment	**Don't** accept rooms, spaces and places as they are.	**Do** take every opportunity to shape an atmosphere that is likely to make people feel comfortable and relaxed.
5. Be body conscious	**Don't** ignore the sensations that are happening in your own body.	**Do** notice what is happening to you and what it may be saying about your situation or other people.

Appendix

The ten principles of emotional literacy

Principle	Don't	Do
6. Recognise your role	**Don't** be quick to blame another person.	**Do** observe your own role in any situation and stop to think about the influence you may have had in shaping it.
7. Value people	**Don't** rush to judge, label or stereotype.	**Do** keep an open mind about people as you listen to what they are saying.
8. Intervene early	**Don't** leave a situation to brew until emotions have become complex and difficult.	**Do** keep a watchful eye out for signs of emotional heat, and intervene as early as you can.
9. Acknowledge when your own emotional state mirrors that of your students	**Don't** pretend that you are not affected by what you experience.	**Do** acknowledge what you are feeling and, when it feels right, share that information with your colleagues or your students.
10. Make it possible for people to change themselves	**Don't** try hectoring, cajoling or pushing people to change in ways that you think will be good for them.	**Do** make it possible for people to explore with you the ways they might want to change and how they might do that.

Useful organisations

These organisations *all* provide training in emotional literacy for people working in schools. Some of them also provide consultancy and other services.

Antidote
www.antidote.org.uk *(Offers the PROGRESS programme to shape emotionally literate cultures to support learning through wellbeing)*

Family Links
www.familylinks.org.uk

Institute of Arts Therapy and Education
www.artspsychotherapy.org

Jenny Mosley Consultancies
www.circle-time.co.uk *(Circle Time training)*

Marilyn Tew and Partners
www.marilyntew.co.uk
(Circle Time and tutor training)

Osiris Educational
www.osiriseducational.co.uk
(Circle Time training and RTime)

RTime
www.rtime.info/courses_accredited.htm

The Place2Be
www.theplace2be.org.uk

Sapere
www.sapere.org.uk *(Philosophy for children)*

School of Emotional Literacy
www.schoolofemotional-literacy.com

Sowelu Associates
www.soweluassociates.co.uk

Transforming Conflict
www.transformingconflict.org
(Restorative justice training and consultancy)

Working with Others
www.workingwithothers.org
(Groupwork training)

Useful books

Circle Time for Emotional Literacy
by Sue Roffey
Published by Paul Chapman, 2006

Circles, PSHE and Citizenship
by Marilyn Tew, Mary Read & Hilary Potter
Published by Sage, 2007

*Creativity: Flow and the Psychology
of Discovery and Invention*
by Mihaly Csikszentmihalyi
Published by Harper/Perennial, 1997

*Descartes' Error: Emotion, Reason and the
Human Brain* by Antonio Damasio
Published by Grosset/Putnam, 1995

Developing the Emotionally Literate School
by Katherine Weare
Published by Sage, 2003

*Emotional Literacy Handbook: Promoting
whole-school strategies*
by Antidote
Published by Fulton, 2004

*Emotional Literacy at the Heart
of School Ethos* by Steve Killick
Published by Sage, 2006

Learning Power in Practice
by Ruth Deakin-Crick
Published by Sage, 2006

Nurturing Emotional Literacy by Peter Sharp
Published by Fulton, 2001

Quality Circle Time in the Secondary School
by Jenny Mosley and Marilyn Tew
Published by Fulton, 1999

*School Effectiveness: Student success through
emotional literacy* by Marilyn Tew
Published by Sage, 2007

*Turn Your School Around: Circle-time approach
to the development of self-esteem and positive
behaviour in the primary staffroom, classroom
and playground*
by Jenny Mosley
Published by LDA, 1998

About the authors

James Park

James is the founding director of Antidote, an organisation working with schools to help shape emotional environments that give young people the best possible opportunity to learn and grow. He led the team that developed Antidote Environment for Learning Survey (ELS), a research-validated tool for measuring emotional literacy and wellbeing. He was the editor of *Raising Achievement Update* from 2003 to 2008.

Marilyn Tew

Marilyn's career in education has taken her into many different contexts. She has worked in pre-school playgroups, grammar and special schools and as an assistant headteacher in a large comprehensive. She worked for ten years as a freelance consultant and trainer before becoming development director at Antidote. Her books include *School Effectiveness: Student success through emotional literacy* and (with Hilary Potter & Mary Read) *Circles, PSHE and Citizenship: The value of circle time in secondary schools.*

Order form

Your details

Name _____

Position _____

School _____

Address _____

_____

Telephone _____

Fax _____

E-mail _____

VAT No. (EC only) _____

Your Order Ref _____

Please send me:

		No. Copies
Emotional Literacy _____	Pocketbook	
_____	Pocketbook	
_____	Pocketbook	
_____	Pocketbook	
_____	Pocketbook	

Order by Post

Teachers' Pocketbooks

Laurel House, Station Approach
Alresford, Hants. SO24 9JH UK

Order by Phone, Fax or Internet

Telephone: +44 (0)1962 735573
Facsimile: +44 (0)1962 733637
E-mail: sales@teacherspocketbooks.co.uk
Web: www.teacherspocketbooks.co.uk